S0-BOS-446

# Chinese Kites

## How to Make and Fly Them

# CHINESE KITES
## How to Make and Fly Them

by David F. Jue

**CHARLES E. TUTTLE COMPANY**
Rutland, Vermont & Tokyo, Japan

*Representatives*
*For Continental Europe:*
BOXERBOOKS, INC., *Zurich*
*For the British Isles:*
PRENTICE-HALL INTERNATIONAL, INC., *London*
*For Australasia:*
PAUL FLESCH & CO., PTY. LTD., *Melbourne*
*For Canada:*
M. G. HURTIG LTD., *Edmonton*



*Published by the Charles E. Tuttle Company, Inc.*
*of Rutland, Vermont & Tokyo, Japan*
*with editorial offices at*
*Suido 1-chome, 2-6, Bunkyo-ku, Tokyo*



*Library of Congress Catalog Card No. 67-16412*

*International Standard Book No. 0-8048-0101-0*

*First edition, 1967*
*Seventh printing, 1972*

*Book design by Keiko Chiba*

PRINTED IN JAPAN

# Contents

# Introduction

David F. Jue (rhymes with "dew") was born in Kwangtung Province in southeastern China, the province in which the city of Canton is located. He migrated to America at the age of fourteen.

Facing the challenge of a new life, he earned money for his education and prospered as a salesman in California. During the many years of his residence in Fresno, I came to know this gentleman intimately. He retired in 1948 and made his home in Palo Alto, but his abundant energy found no outlet. He joined the brokerage office of Sutro & Co., retiring again in 1963.

Beside an avenue near his Palo Alto home, Mr. Jue noticed a fine clump of green bamboo destined to be uprooted in a street-widening project. In the culture of Mr. Jue's boyhood, the bamboo is a pervasive symbol, a gift from nature of grace and beauty—and, to the eminently practical Chinese, a uniquely useful item. This gift of nature was meant to be either cherished or harvested for use. He proceeded to rescue the bamboo from the indignity of the bulldozer and the waste of the trash heap.

What more natural than that the feel of the bamboo in his hands should recall pleasant memories from his boyhood—and that kite-making should be one of them? Mr. Jue had found a new and consuming interest in life. He began making kites as he remembered them of old, eventually inventing new designs and adapting the old techniques to the materials at hand in his community.

A soaring kite, beautifully formed and painted, with colorful streaming tails, is a striking sight in this increasingly mechanical and prosaic age. The children of the neighborhood flocked about whenever Mr. Jue lofted his kites and soon joined in the fun. Inevitably, they invaded his workshop and joined in the fun of making and painting the kites, as well.

Mr. Jue's personal diversion had gained a new dimension. Teaching children and sharing their unreserved delight at a first launching was more fun than merely making kites for his own amusement. And the sudden upsurge of interest in an exotic handicraft and constructive sport soon leaped the boundaries of Mr. Jue's neighborhood. Feature articles appeared in the newspapers of Palo Alto, San Jose, and San Francisco. Schools and department stores invited Mr. Jue to give demonstrations. Hundreds of inquiries came by mail and telephone. The spreading interest in Chinese kite-making has encouraged Mr. Jue in his effort to bring an ancient and rewarding folk-art to the youth of his adopted land.

by JOHN D. ROMANO

# Chinese Kites
## How to Make and Fly Them

# The History of Kites

Kites were in use in China long before the beginnings of written history. Bamboo for frames was native to the land. Silk has been produced in China since stone-age times, as long ago as 2600 B.C. With bamboo available for frames and silk for the coverings and the flying lines, the art of kite-making arose as an amusement and as an adjunct of the primitive religions. By the beginning of historical times, kites were already widely used from Korea to Southeast Asia.

According to a Chinese legend, the Chinese people of the Han dynasty were saved from being conquered by a barbarian army through ingenious use of a kite. A certain Huan Theng, a great scholar and advisor to the emperor, was called upon for a plan to defeat or rout the superior forces of the invader.

Huan Theng put his clever mind to work. The palace walls were vulnerable only from one side, so the enemy forces were deployed only in one direction from the palace. As Huan Theng stood on the ramparts, surveying the scene and pondering the problem, his hat was lifted off by the strong, steady wind and sailed away across the fields. In Huan Theng's quick mind, the problem was solved. He advised the emperor to cause a number of kites to be made. Huang Theng busied himself making a number of special sounding devices. He trimmed a piece of bamboo very, very thin, and tied each end to a bow-shaped twig and attached it to the top of the kite.

In the darkest, eeriest time of the night, the kites were lofted above the positions of the enemy. The wind vibrating the sounding devices produced sounds like low moans and high-pitched wails. Spies sent into the enemy lines spread the word that

WWHHHZZZZZEEEEE

the gods were warning them that they would be destroyed. The enemy fled in terror.

Huang Theng may well have used paper to cover his kites. The origin of paper in China has been traced back at least as far as 200 B.C., when the Han dynasty was young. When paper became commonplace, the cheaper material put kite-making into the reach of all. The kite, probably first a jealously guarded stratagem of the primitive priest-magician and then the expensive toy of the wealthy, became a folk art of the people and as such survives today.

Widespread kite-making among the people insured the transmission of the art from generation to generation. Time and again the people found protection in the use of kites. About A.D. 500, Emperor Liang Moo used kites as signals to rally his soldiers in time of danger. A large army could not be kept constantly at the palace. They were allowed to disperse to work their farms. When danger threatened, kites were flown from high points across the countryside as a signal to assemble at the palace. Once when the enemy had closed in quickly and surrounded the palace, the emperor directed his commander, Gan Mon, to loft the kites. In response, kites arose from point after point across the land. The army assembled at a distance and attacked the enemy from the rear, routing them utterly.

Kites have also been used for individual or family protection. Using a sounding device similar to that of Huan Theng, or a sort of flute made from perforated reed or bamboo, kites were lofted over the house throughout the night to frighten away thieves and bandits. The more superstitious continue this practice to protect the house from the evil spirits of the night.

## Fishing with Kites

People go fishing in china, just as they do here. Those who can afford it have boats; others just sit on the banks of the river or lake. On a breezy day, you may see kites flying above the water with a long string tied to the tail. At the end of this string, a hook with the bait is submerged under the water. When a fish bites, the fisherman pulls the kite in. This sight is very common around lakes and rivers.

# Firecracker Scarecrows

On remotely placed farms where numerous birds to invade the crops, farmers often have their children fly kites with firecrackers tied to the tails. Slow burning incense attached to the fuses sets off the firecrackers at intervals, scaring the birds away.

## Centipede Kite

One of the largest kites made in China is the centipede kite. The Chinese word for the centipede also means "One Hundred Legs." This kite ranges in size from a few feet to fifty feet and longer. The centipede's body is made of ring-shaped bamboo frames covered with colored paper and strung together, a foot or more apart, one after another. Bamboo sticks cross the upper third of the frames, and protrude six inches beyond the edges. On both ends of each stick streamers of colored paper represent legs. Four strings run the length of the centipede's body, one attached to the protruding stick on each side and one along top and bottom, hold all the circles together. When this kite is in the air, the individual parts wiggle in the breeze, making the centipede seem alive. The head is five or six times larger than the body frames. As the frames near the tail, they grow smaller. The end frame is sometimes only about the size of a silver dollar coin. It is necessary to have heavy twine and, in the case of a very large centipede kite, a team of men to control its flight. The flight of a huge centipede kite in the sky is indeed a spectacular sight!

# The Festival of Ascending on High

The Chinese meteorologists discovered long ago that easterly winds usually prevail during the first part of September, creating a more ideal weather for kite-flying than at any other time of the year. So the period from the first to the ninth of September was established as The Festival of Ascending on High. After school, students fly kites of all shapes and designs. On the ninth day of the festival, the schools declare a holiday so that all of the pupils can fly their kites to their hearts' content. At the end of the day, when one is finished flying his kite, one lets the kite go, string and all. All of the evil, bad luck, and sickness are carried away with the kite. Custom requires that whoever finds the kite after it has fallen to the ground must burn it, just as we burn Christmas trees after Christmas.

# Kite Fights

Kite fighting is very popular in China and is the most exciting sport of the kite-flying season. Each participant puts special care into the design and construction of his kite to obtain the utmost stability and maneuverability. He coats about a hundred feet of the flying line, nearest the kite, with glue and applies powdered glass or sand. This provides an abrasive surface which he will use to attempt to saw through the flying line of his adversary. It is also a defense against his line being sawed by his opponent.

The decoration of these kites is something to behold! Each is painted to represent the most ferocious, frightening demon that the owner can imagine. The more scarey the decoration, the better are the owner's chances of victory!

The contestants loft their kites, then take up positions from forty to sixty feet apart. The kites are flown at a much lower angle to the ground than normally. At this low angle, they tend to dart and dodge in fast swoops. The object is to engage the strings, try to maintain a more vigorous sawing motion with the flying line than one's opponent, be careful not to lose the lift of the wind, and saw the opponent's flying line in two. The victor obtains right of ownership of the vanquished kite.

In another and easier version of the kite fight, the object is to entangle the flying lines, maneuver to cause the opponent's kite to lose lift, and haul it in dangling from one's own flying line.

# The Fertility Kite

Rice is the staple food of the millions living in southern China. With the average farmer, the rice crop is not to sell for cash but for consumption by his family. A good crop means survival for another year.

When the farmer's son comes of age, the farmer presents him with a "rice kite" to fly over his newly assigned rice paddies. The design and shape of the kite are not important, but a sheaf of unthreshed rice is attached to dangle head down from each side and another sheaf is tied to the tail. As the kite is lofted over the son's paddies, the action of the wind shakes the rice grains from the straw, sprinkling them over the ground. If he can keep the kite aloft until all of the grains have dropped, he is assured of bountiful crops from this land henceforth.

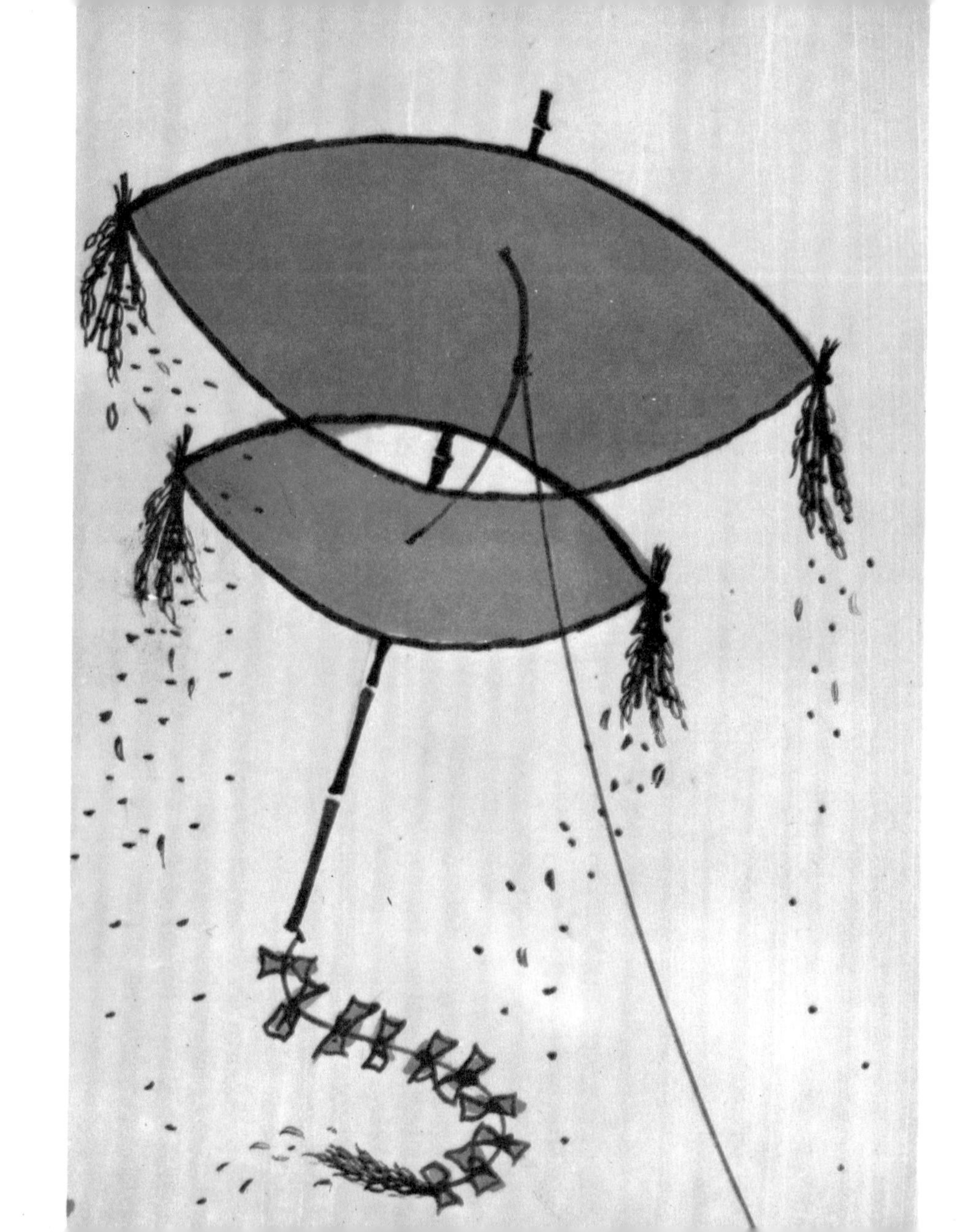

# Making Your Own Chinese Kite

## Materials and Where to Get Them

**Split bamboo** is the most suitable material for kite frames. It is both light and strong. Tough and flexible, it can be bent into loops which will retain their shapes. A very convenient source of bamboo, already split and practically ready for use, is available everywhere today at a very nominal cost. Most stores selling outdoor furniture also sell shades made of split bamboo. Locally, I have been able to buy them at Sears Roebuck, Montgomery Ward, and Thrift Drugstores. For example, I am now using strips from some that I bought for 89 cents each. A shade 26″ high and 48″ wide contains about 50 lengths of split bamboo, enough for as many as 15 kites. While these strips should be shaved down a bit for the smaller kites to eliminate weight, I use them just as they are for the larger kites. I also am using bamboo from a 72″ × 144″ shade which cost $3.50. From this shade I can make at least 200 butterfly kites. This size is most economical, less than 2 cents per kite frame, and is an especially good source for hobby centers, schools, or any organized group. Look for shades in which the width of the strips is .25 to .4 inches, .5 inches at the most.

In addition, each shade has a round section of bamboo at top and bottom which can be split once and used for center posts.

**Rice paper** is best for covering kite frames. It also is light, strong, and tough. When dry it is as tough as cloth and much lighter in weight. It is easily torn or punctured when wet, but dries quickly becoming as tough as before. Since decorating with water colors wets the paper, reasonable care not to punch the brush through the paper and an adequate drying period before flying are necessary. But the virtues of rice paper so outweigh this factor that I can not honestly recommend any substitute that I have tried.

Practically any stationery store or art supply shop, including such counters in the department stores, can sell you good quality rice paper at reasonable cost. I have been paying 25 to 30 cents for a 40″ by 24″ sheet. Such a sheet will cover any kite described in this book and will cover two of the smaller types such as the redtail hawk or butterfly.

**Tying string** for securing the joints of the kite frame is not a very critical item. Common 4-ply cotton string such as stores once used to wrap packages is suitable. A heavy gauge sewing thread is also good, if you make a few more turns for strength, and it makes neater knots. You want strength without bulk and without stretch. Here, common sense should be an adequate guide.

**Glue** for securing the joints of the kite frame may be any type which dries rapidly to a tough, rather than brittle, condition. I recommend one of the white glues such as Elmer's Glue-All, by Borden, or Carter's Nu-Glu.

**Paints** for decorating the cover may be whatever you like to use. Watercolors and poster paints are easy for the novice painter. If you are new to such decorating, I suggest that you go to any art supply outlet, explain what you want to do, and obtain the brushes and paints recommended to you for the purpose.

**Tails** are usually made from the same cord used in the flying line with rag strips about 2 inches wide and 6 inches long tied in at 6-inch intervals. But you may also use a rag strip or cloth tape instead of cord. Where the kite needs a double tail, use a crepe paper tape of the type used for holiday room-decoration.

**Flying line and Bridle** must be as strong as the size of your kite demands and as light in weight as the strength requirement permits. For the smaller kites, I pay 10 cents for a 275-foot ball of 3-ply, 6 lb-test twine called "Household and Kite Twine." For the larger kites, I buy a 16 lb-test cable cord which comes in 200-foot rolls.

**Reels** for flying lines can be made in a simple but useful form from soft wood. Some shapes are illustrated above. Similar reels made of heavy wire are sold in toy stores.

## Tools Required

**Knives** used in working with bamboo should have a heavy, inflexible, short blade, and a thick handle upon which you can get a good grip. The blade must be of high-quality steel which will take a keen edge. You should keep the blade very sharp. More accidents happen when using dull knives than with sharp knives.

**Saws** are handy for cutting bamboo strips into proper lengths. A small saw with fine teeth in cross-cut arrangement works best with bamboo.

**Scissors** are needed for cutting string and trimming rice paper for covers. Any good pair of paper shears will be suitable.

**A ruler** is handy to have for measuring bamboo lengths and drawing designs on covers.

**Pencils** are needed for drawing outlines of kite cover design prior to painting. A fairly soft-leaded drawing pencil or common lead-pencil is suitable.

**Paint brushes** used will depend upon type of paints used and you can be advised by sales persons at the art supply store. But you must remember that you will be painting upon a finished kite and that the rice paper upon which you are painting will not be supported by a flat surface. Since rice paper tears rather easily when wet, your brush must be soft and flexible.

# General Techniques

## Making Kite Frame

Select strips of split bamboo for each component of the frame. Remember that *the kite must be balanced*. Strips for symmetrical positions on the left and right of the kite should be as nearly as possible of the same overall weight. Crosspieces should be as even as possible in cross-section from one end to the other. Overall weight can be compared roughly by simply placing strips side by side and matching dimensions. Or, you can compare weights on a simple balance. Evenness from one end to the other can be insured by measuring across the width with a ruler at points among the length.

Soak those strips which must be bent in water for an hour or two, so that they will bend without breaking.

Assemble the frame in the sequence indicated in the instructions.

Cut tying string into 6-inch lengths. Where bamboo strips cross each other, make at least two turns with string through both diagonals of the crossing point. Where bamboo strips are to be spliced together in parallel position, make two ties as far apart as the arrangement permits. Tie off with a square-knot. If you are not sure that you make a real square-knot, tie the knot twice to be sure it will not slip. Clip off excess string neatly.

Check the balance of the kite. Always do this before gluing the knots. The critical balance involves the weight on each side of the vertical axis, or centerpole. Rest one tip of the centerpole on the edge of a table and support the other tip upon your finger with the kite resting in a horizontal plane. If the kite tends to rotate, with one side tipping down and the other rising up, one side is heavier than the other.

When the kite is flying, there are two elements involved in balance: (1) weight distribution on each side of the centerpole. (2) surface area against which the wind presses and its distribution on each side of the centerpole. If the kite does not balance, first take measurements to insure that the centerpole is in the center of what will become the kite's surface area. Loosen knots and adjust centerpole position, if necessary. If centerpole is found to be accurately centered, the imbalance is due to the weight of bamboo strips on one side being greater than those on the other. Inspect strips for excessively thick areas on the heavy side and reduce weight by whittling away the excess thickness. Since you want the frame to be as light as possible, I do not recommend adjusting balance by adding counterweight to the light side.

When you are certain that the positions of the bamboo strips are correct, apply glue to the joints and knots. Use just enough glue to soak the string thoroughly. When the glue has dried, you will have a rigid kite frame which will stand the stresses and vibrations of flying. Generally, it is best not to continue work on the kite until glue has dried.

## Covering Kite Frame

Place a sheet of rice paper on a table and position the completed frame so that the paper will cover the desired areas. Trace around the outside perimeter of the frame areas, leaving a margin of ½ inch for overlap. Then cut out the traced shape with your paper shears.

Position the frame on the cut-out paper in such manner that the centerpole is the uppermost component of the frame. Apply white glue to the margins of the rice paper and fold the margins back over the bamboo, or string, portions of the frame.

## Decorating Kite Cover

The color pictures of kite decoration provided in this book will serve as a guide in making your kite really look Chinese. Note the bright colors and the combinations of colors. Where the kite represents a living creature, note the use of color to enhance and emphasize the basic patterns of nature. Of course you do not have to copy these designs slavishly. You are quite free to exercise your own creative talents—and you will certainly enjoy this part of kite-making more if you do so.

Before you start to decorate the kite, remember to spread some old newspapers, wrapping paper, canvas, etc., on the table or floor to catch any paint that spills or drips through the rice paper.

When applying the paints, the rice paper necessarily becomes wet. It will tear easily, so you must paint with gentle strokes. Also, the paper will sag when wet. Do not worry about this. It will draw tight on the frame again when it dries.

Do not continue work on the kite until paper dries.

## Making and Attaching the Tail

All flat kites need tails. Without a tail, the kite would loop and spin beyond the control of the most expert handler. A tail is not needed on the flying lampshade because the combination of its 3-dimensional airframe with its low point of attachment to the flying line is naturally stable. The same applies to the conventional box kite.

The tail provides stability by virtue of both its weight and its air-resistance. A well-designed tail limits the movements of the kite in response to changes of wind pressure and direction but does not suppress the lifelike grace of the kite's dance with the wind. And a good tail also dances. If the tail is too long, too heavy, or too inflexible, the tail will "wag the kite." If the tail is too short, the kite will loop and spin.

The tail requirements vary with the size and shape of the kite and also with wind conditions. The average kite in normal conditions performs best with from 10 to 15 feet of tail. A very large kite, or a small kite on a very windy day, may need a 25-foot tail.

The standard single kite tail is made by knotting strips of cloth into a strong cord at intervals. Using strips about 2″ × 6″ cut from rags or cloth tape, knot the cord about the center of the cloth strip so that the strip stands out equally to each side of the length of cord. If you knot the strip to the cord, the strips will slide down the cord and end up in a bundle. An interval of about six inches between strips is usually best. The performance of both kite and tail can be adjusted in two ways: (1) by shortening or lengthening the tail. (2) by changing the interval between strips.

A variation on this standard tail is made using a long strip of cloth or cloth tape instead of the cord. In this case, the short cloth strips can be knotted about the center strip without slippage, if tightly knotted.

Some kite designs look more natural with double tails. The butterfly, redtail hawk, and fish kites are good examples. The standard-type tails in a double arrangement, would tend to tangle. For the double tail, use lengths of crepe paper with no strips tied in. Crepe-paper tails are attached by gluing, rather than tying.

In the beginning, you can save much time and trouble by preparing several tails of different lengths and weights and taking them with you to the flying field.

## Bridles

Flat kites also need a bridle arrangement to control the angle at which the surface meets the wind. The wind lifts the kite by being diverted downward along the face of the kite. Since the kite is not free to go with the wind, the wind pushes the kite upwards as it escapes past the lower edge. The bridle controls the angle at which the kite faces the wind.

A basic bridle consists of two legs only. One leg is tied to the upper portion of the

centerpole, the other to the lower portion. At any given moment of flight, one leg will be serving primarily as an extension of the flying line while the other acts as a guy-line to keep the proper angle. The optimum points of attachment to centerpole and lengths of legs cannot be prescribed here. These will vary with each kite according to materials used, tail design and length, and strength of wind. The bridling and tail arrangements must be adjusted to the kite and the wind. One tends to compensate the other.

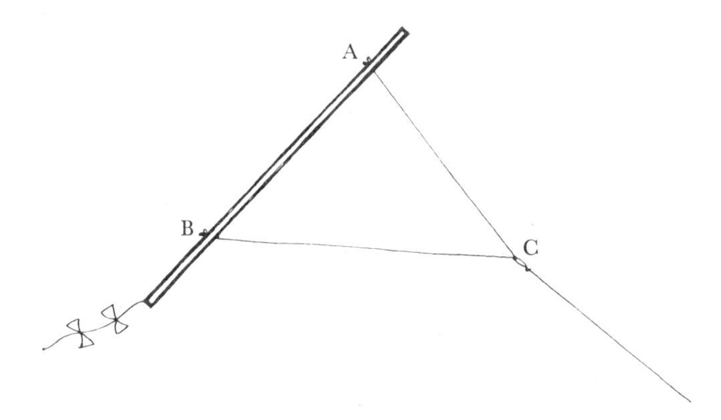


A basic bridle arrangement is shown above. Bridles are attached after frame has been decorated, as follows:

STEP 1: Select points of attachment. Using nail or other round-pointed tool, punch small holes in cover. If, in punching holes, a tear starts, apply one of the little doughnut-shape reinforcing rings designed for pages in looseleaf notebooks.

STEP 2: Cut a length of flying line about four times as long as distance AB. Insert one end through upper hole and tie to centerpole with bowknot or clove hitch.

STEP 3: Measure back along bridle (AC) a distance equal to AB and tie a small loop.

STEP 4: Insert remaining end through lower hole. Holding AC straight out from kite, pull CB through hole until slack is removed. Tie to centerpole with bowknot or clove hitch. The excess should be retained for possible later adjustments.

If the design of the frame permits attaching bridle at points where frame crosses centerpole, the ties will not slip and tear cover. If tied with clove hitch, ties will not slip.

The relative length of bridle legs can be adjusted by loosening and shifting the loop. If points of attachment must be shifted up or down the centerpole, bowknots or clove hitcher can be easily untied. Old holes in cover should be patched with scotch tape.

## Launching Your Kite

Buildings and trees break the force of the wind, so it is best to fly your kite from an open field. The fewer trees there are, the less chance there will be of losing your kite in one of them.

Unroll fifty to seventy-five feet of line. If you can get a helper, have him hold the kite as high as he can. If the kite has a tail, it should stretch away from you, on the ground, directly behind the kite. In this position, it will help to balance the kite as it rises into the air.

As your helper releases the kite, back up slowly until the kite begins to rise, then gradually let out more line. If the first try at launching is unsuccessful, next time try unrolling more, or less, string.

If you have no helper, you can still launch your kite. If there is a good wind, and your kite is small, stand with your back to the wind, holding the kite by its lower corner or edge. When the wind is steady, toss the kite gently upwards and step backward quickly. As the kite starts to rise, let the line out slowly, keeping it taut. If you feed too much line too quickly, the kite will fall.

If the wind is strong enough and you have followed these instructions, but you still have difficulty getting the kite into the air, try re-adjusting the bridle or changing the length of the tail.

# Kite Designs and Instructions

## Orange Kite

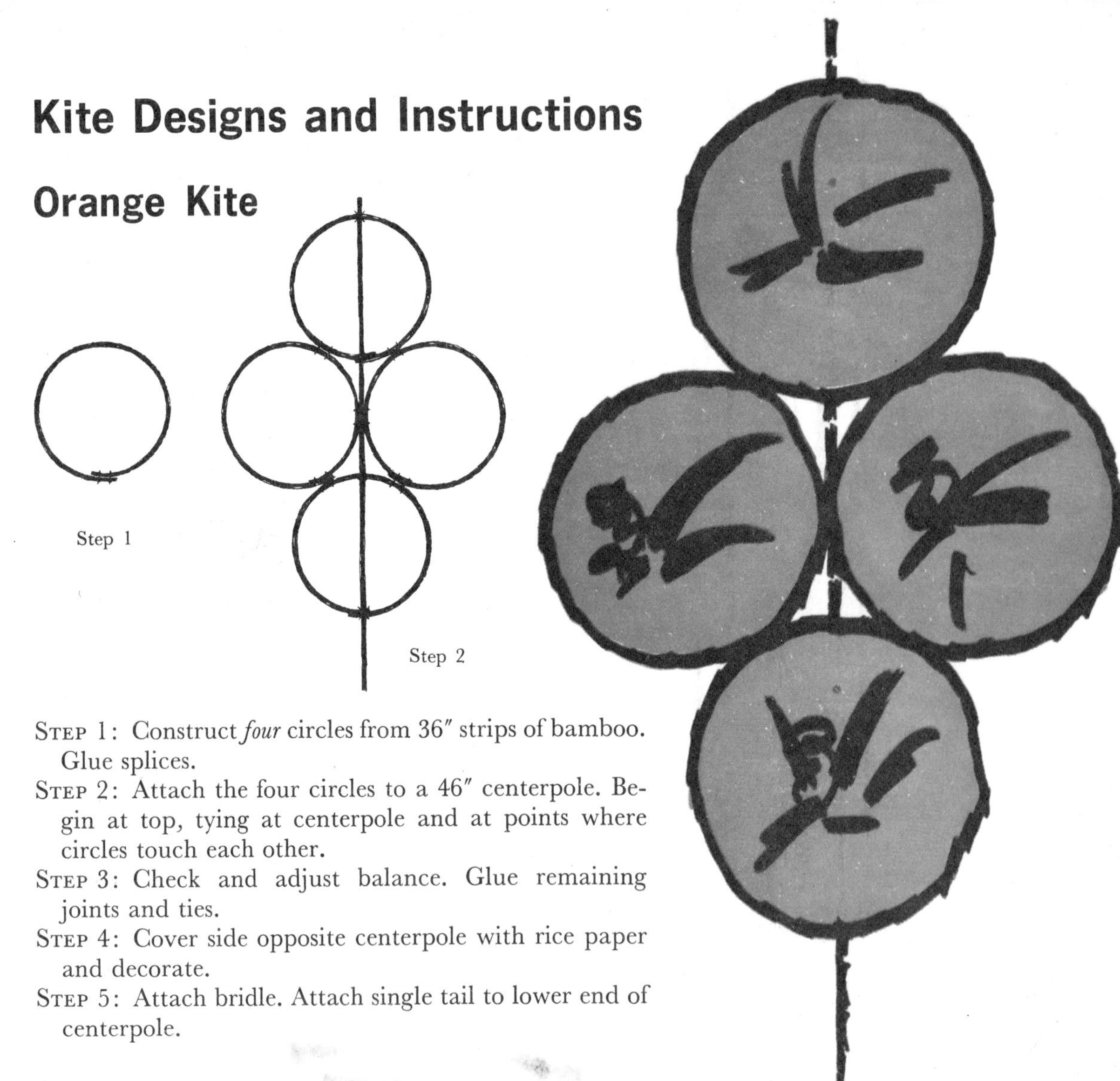


STEP 1: Construct *four* circles from 36″ strips of bamboo. Glue splices.

STEP 2: Attach the four circles to a 46″ centerpole. Begin at top, tying at centerpole and at points where circles touch each other.

STEP 3: Check and adjust balance. Glue remaining joints and ties.

STEP 4: Cover side opposite centerpole with rice paper and decorate.

STEP 5: Attach bridle. Attach single tail to lower end of centerpole.

# Pine Tree Kite

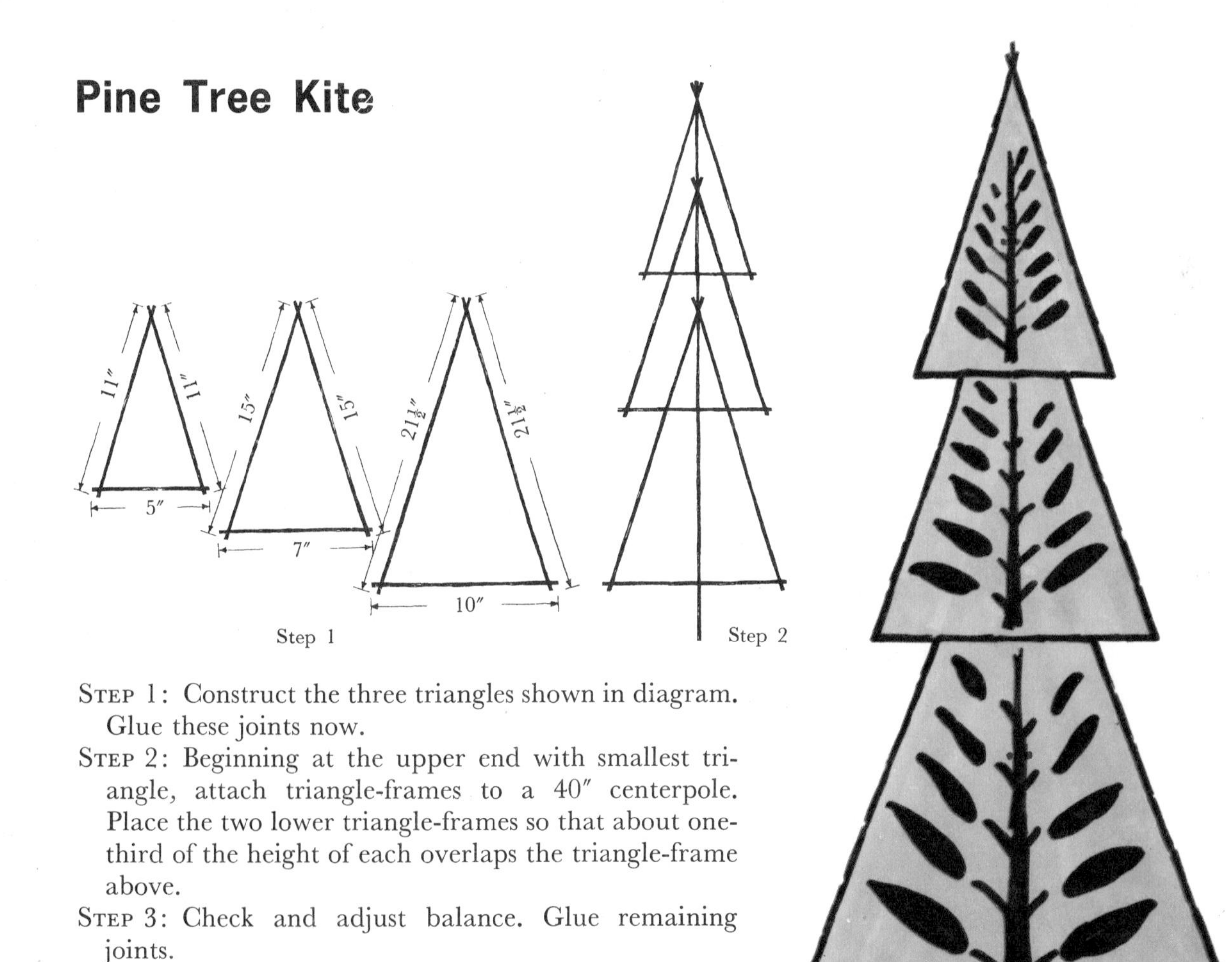


STEP 1: Construct the three triangles shown in diagram. Glue these joints now.

STEP 2: Beginning at the upper end with smallest triangle, attach triangle-frames to a 40″ centerpole. Place the two lower triangle-frames so that about one-third of the height of each overlaps the triangle-frame above.

STEP 3: Check and adjust balance. Glue remaining joints.

STEP 4: Cover side opposite centerpole with rice paper and decorate.

STEP 5: Attach bridle. Attach single tail to lower end of centerpole.

# Schoolhouse Kite

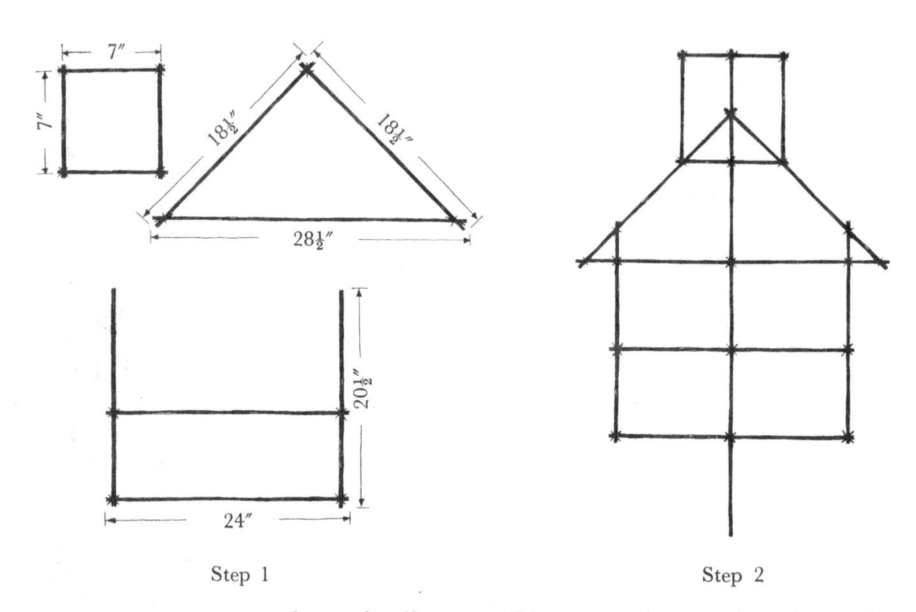


STEP 1: Construct components shown in diagram. The center brace of the lower figure should be tied only temporarily, using bowknots. Its position will be determined in step 2.

STEP 2: Beginning at the top, with the 7″ square, assemble the components to a 40″ centerpole. The positioning of each figure will be determined, in turn, by key points marked "k" on diagram. Tie all joints of assembly. Loosen bowknots holding center brace of lower figure; adjust to position halfway between lower edge of roof and lower crossbrace. Now, tie joints permanently.

STEP 3: Check and adjust balance of frame. Glue all joints.

STEP 4: Cover side opposite centerpole with rice paper and decorate.

STEP 5: Attach bridle. Attach single tail to lower end of centerpole.

# Octagon Kite

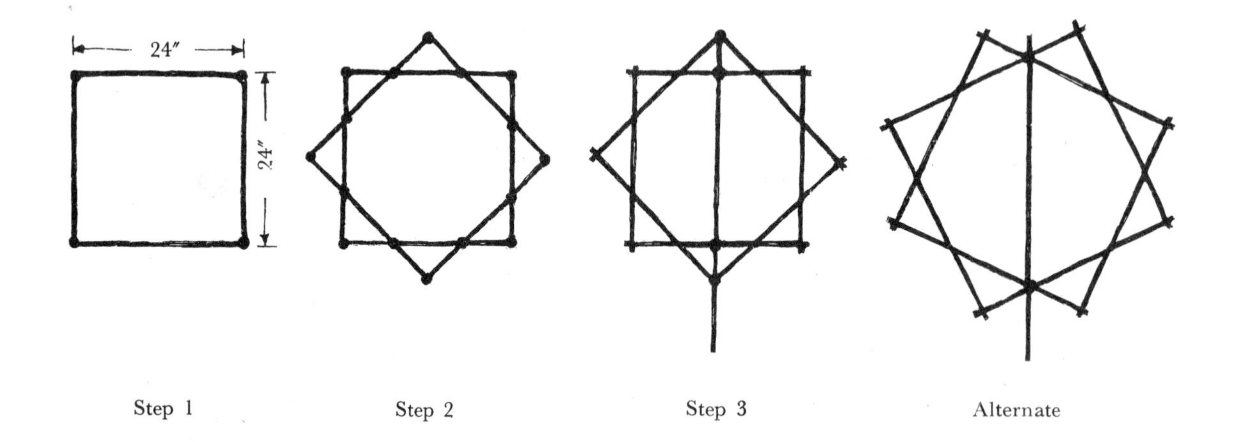


Step 1 Step 2 Step 3 Alternate

STEP 1: Construct *two* square frames as indicated.

STEP 2: Place one square atop the other in the position shown. Bend top square and tuck upper and lower corners beneath the upper and lower sides of the other square. The squares are now interlaced into one structure. Carefully adjust points so that all triangles around the outer edge are equal in size; then tie *and glue* all joints.

STEP 3: Attach 40″ centerpole in either of the two positions shown.

STEP 4: Check and adjust balance. Glue remaining joints.

STEP 5: Cover side opposite centerpole with rice paper and decorate.

STEP 6: Attach bridle. Attach single tail to lower end of centerpole.

天下太平

# Tree Kite

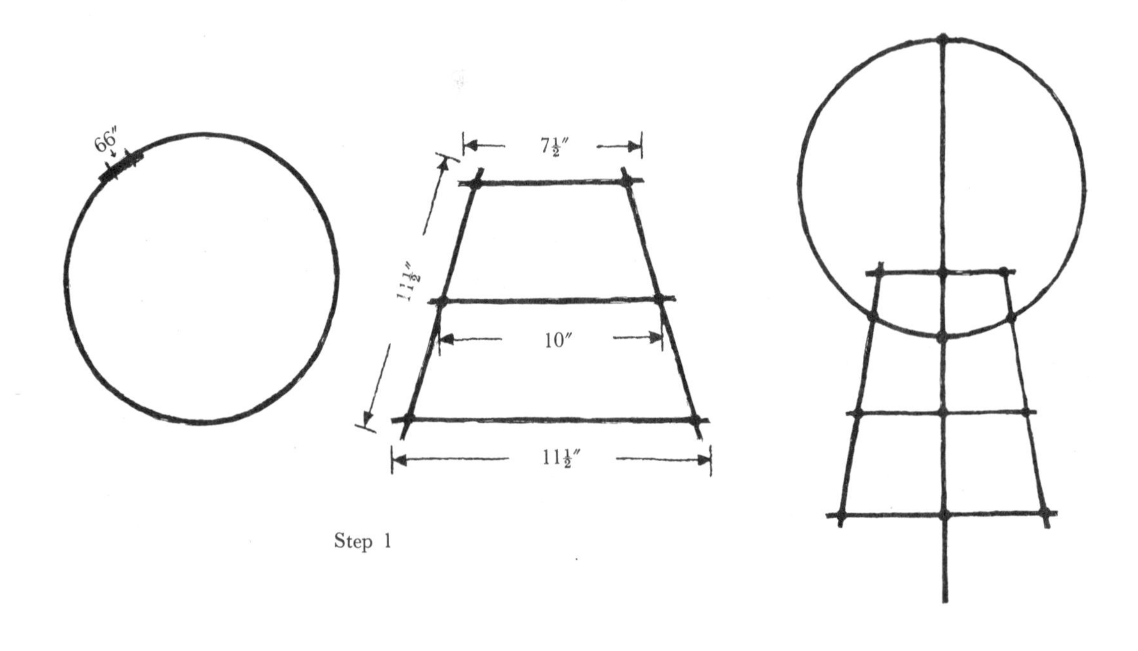

Step 1

Step 2

STEP 1: Construct components shown in diagram.
STEP 2: Beginning at the upper end, attach these components to a 36″ centerpole. Overlap the lower figure about two inches into the circle.
STEP 3: Check and adjust balance. Glue all joints.
STEP 4: Cover side opposite centerpole with rice paper and decorate.
STEP 5: Attach bridle. Attach single tail to lower end of centerpole.

# Butterfly Kite

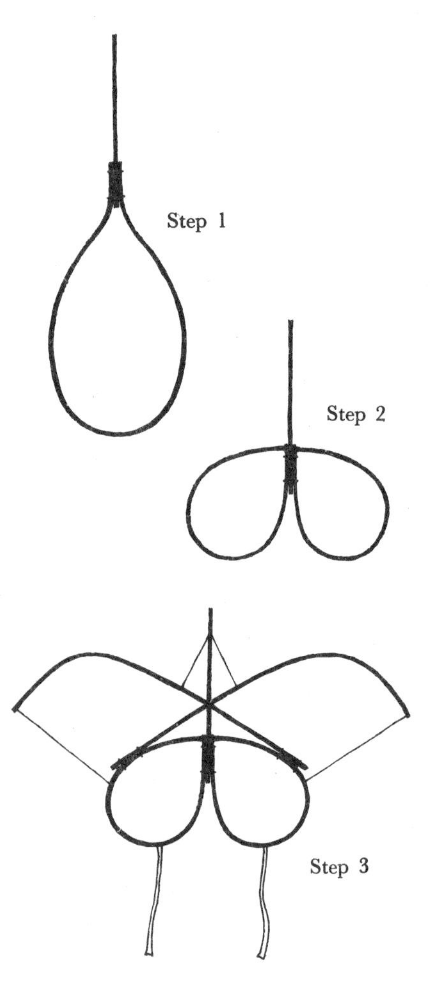


STEP 1: Mark the mid-point of a 48″ length of bamboo. With skin side inward, bend into loop and splice tips to one end of an 18″ bamboo strip. Allow about 6″ overlap.

STEP 2: Bend loop into figure shown. While bending, bamboo will twist bringing skin side outward on the loop. Tie loop to end of spliced section, centering loop on mark made in step 1. If the two resulting loops are not symmetrical due to uneven stiffness of the bamboo, scrape inside surface at stiff areas.

STEP 3: Position two 24″ bamboo strips as shown, crossing 5″ above top of loop. Measure and adjust for equal lengths extending beyond crossing point. Splice to curve of loop on each side and tie at crossing point. Tie a length of string to each wingtip, bend tips inward and tie strings to outer curve of loops at points which create the desired silhouette. Tie a length of string from centerpole to wing on each side to support the paper representing the butterfly's head.

STEP 4: The centerpole of this kite cannot be shifted to adjust weight. Check all dimensions to insure symmetry of area on each side of centerpole. Glue all knots.

STEP 5: Cover side opposite centerpole with rice paper and decorate.

STEP 6: Attach bridle. Attach two 15′ colored crepe-paper tails by gluing to rear surface at lower points.

NOTE: Many additional silhouettes can be created by changing length of wing strips or strings, or by changing points at which tied. Simply be careful to obtain symmetry.

# Redtail Hawk Kite

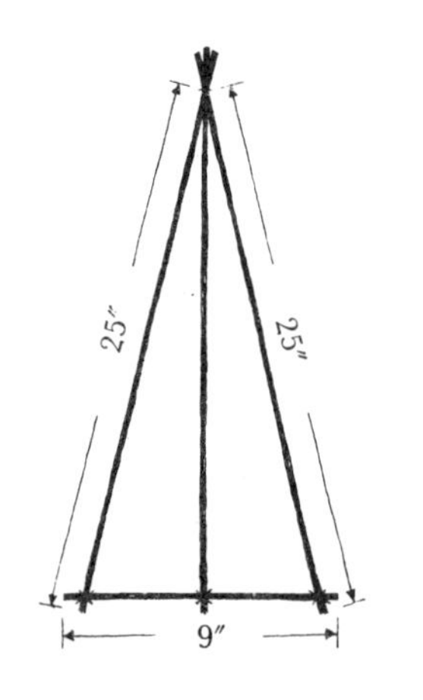


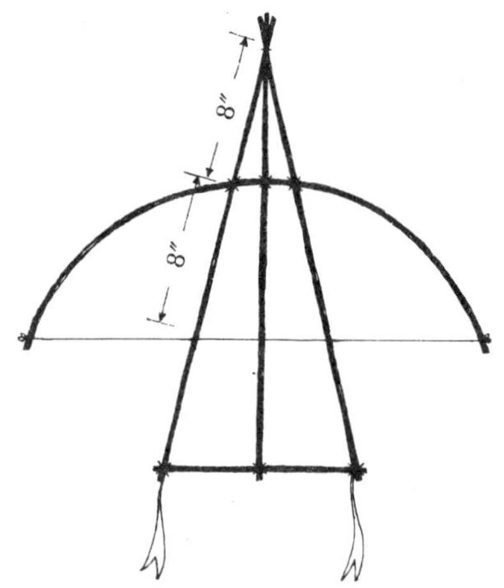


STEP 1: Construct triangle-shaped frame. Attach centerpole.

STEP 2: From top intersection, measure downward about 8″ on each triangle leg and mark. Center a 30″ bamboo strip across these marks on side opposite centerpole. Tie at the three intersections. Measure farther downward about 9″ and mark. Cut a 40″ length of string. Tie to one tip of crosspiece (better to notch bamboo slightly, so will not slip). Bend tip inward until string will stretch horizontally to marks on frame. Make two turns with string around this leg, centerpole, and other leg (both turns should be upward from point of intersection). Bend other tip of crosspiece inward until string will stretch horizontally to it. Tie string with bowknot to notched tip. Do not clip excess string off.

NOTE: The wings may be given a swept-back shape by use of strings between wingtips and lower corners of tail. (This area not to be papered)

STEP 3: Check frame for symmetry. (Distance from wingtip to frame should be equal on each side. Curve of wingtips should be same on each side.) Correct unequal curvature by shaving inner surface of bamboo in any too-rigid areas. Adjust distance from wingtip to frame by slipping string at the turns. Re-adjust length of string, if necessary, to obtain desired curvature of wing.

STEP 4: Check and adjust balance of frame. Convert bowknot at wingtip to square knot. Clip off excess string at wingtip. Glue all joints and string turns.

STEP 5: Cover side opposite centerpole with rice paper and decorate.

STEP 6: Attach bridle. Attach two 15′ colored crepe-paper tails by gluing to the rear surface at the lower corners.

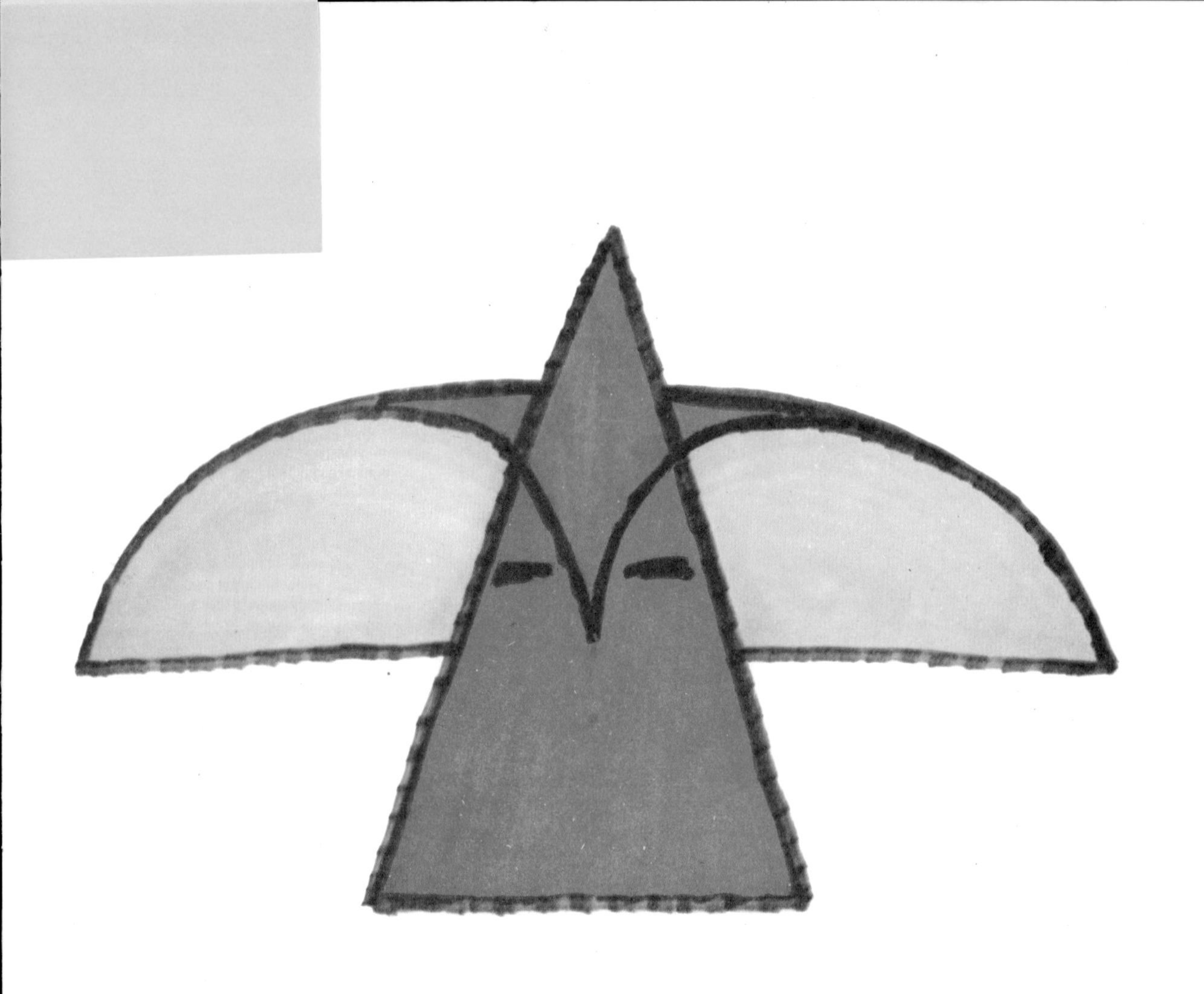

# Three-Deck High Flyer

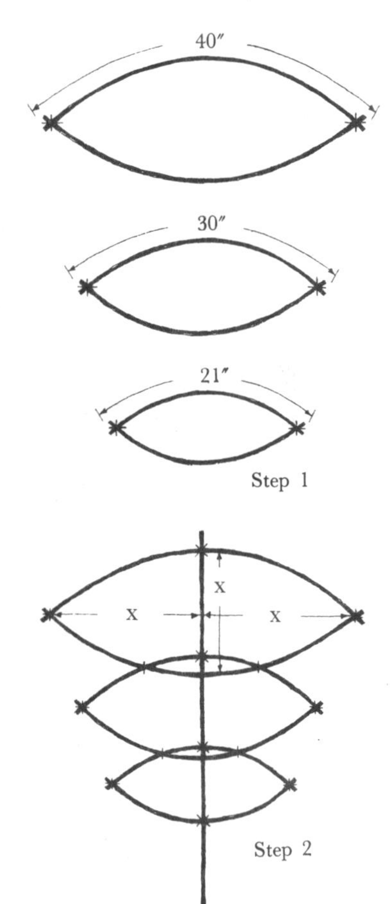

Step 1

Step 2

STEP 1: Construct the components indicated in diagram. After tying tips at one end, place some object between strips so that tips at other end will cross for tying when bent.

STEP 2: Center the longest component across the upper end of a 55″ centerpole. Tie the upper strip tightly to the centerpole about 2″ from upper tip. Mark the center point of the lower strip. Pull lower strip downward until distances marked "x" on diagram are about equal. Tie lower strip tightly to centerpole at the centering mark.

Repeat process with remaining components, overlapping the middle component about 3″ on the upper and the lower about 2″ on the middle component. Tie where curved strips intersect, making certain that points of intersection are equidistant from centerpole.

STEP 3: Check and adjust balance of frame. Glue all joints.

STEP 4: Cover side opposite centerpole with rice paper, leaving space open at overlaps (see colored illustration), and decorate.

STEP 5: Attach bridle. Attach single tail to lower end of centerpole.

# Fish Kite

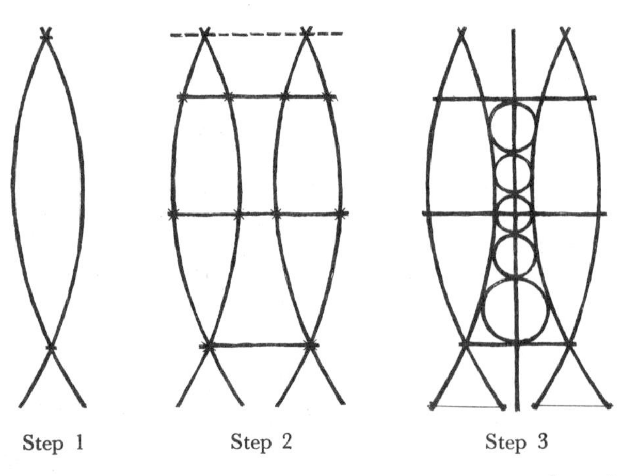


STEP 1: Construct *two* fish-body frames from 38″ bamboo strips. Strips are to be crossed and tied, not spliced parallel. Tie one end at tips, the other 6″ from tips. Place side-by-side and adjust any difference in dimensions.

STEP 2: Attach lower 15″ crosspiece. Attach temporary upper crosspiece as shown by dotted lines (measure to space noses at distance equal to space between tails). Attach 25″ middle crosspiece at measured midpoint of outer fish-body strips. This will spread the fish-body frames into almost symmetrical shapes; but, before tying middle brace to inner strips, measure to insure the two bodies are spread equally. It is important that they be of equal area. Insure that crosspieces are parallel and perpendicular to long axis of fish-bodies. Attach 22″ upper crosspiece at points where its length matches distance between outer fish-body strips. Remove temporary brace from noses.

STEP 3: Attach 40″ centerpole at measured center points of crosspieces on side opposite from fish-body frames. Tie a length of string across the tips of each fish tail.

STEP 4: Check and adjust balance of frame. Glue all knots. Circles are optional and should not affect balance if added later. Bamboo can be bent and cut to fit, beginning at center and adding circles in both directions.

STEP 5: Cover side opposite centerpole with rice paper and decorate.

STEP 6: Attach bridle. Attach single tail to lower end of centerpole, or double tails of colored crepe paper may be glued to outer corner of each fish tail.

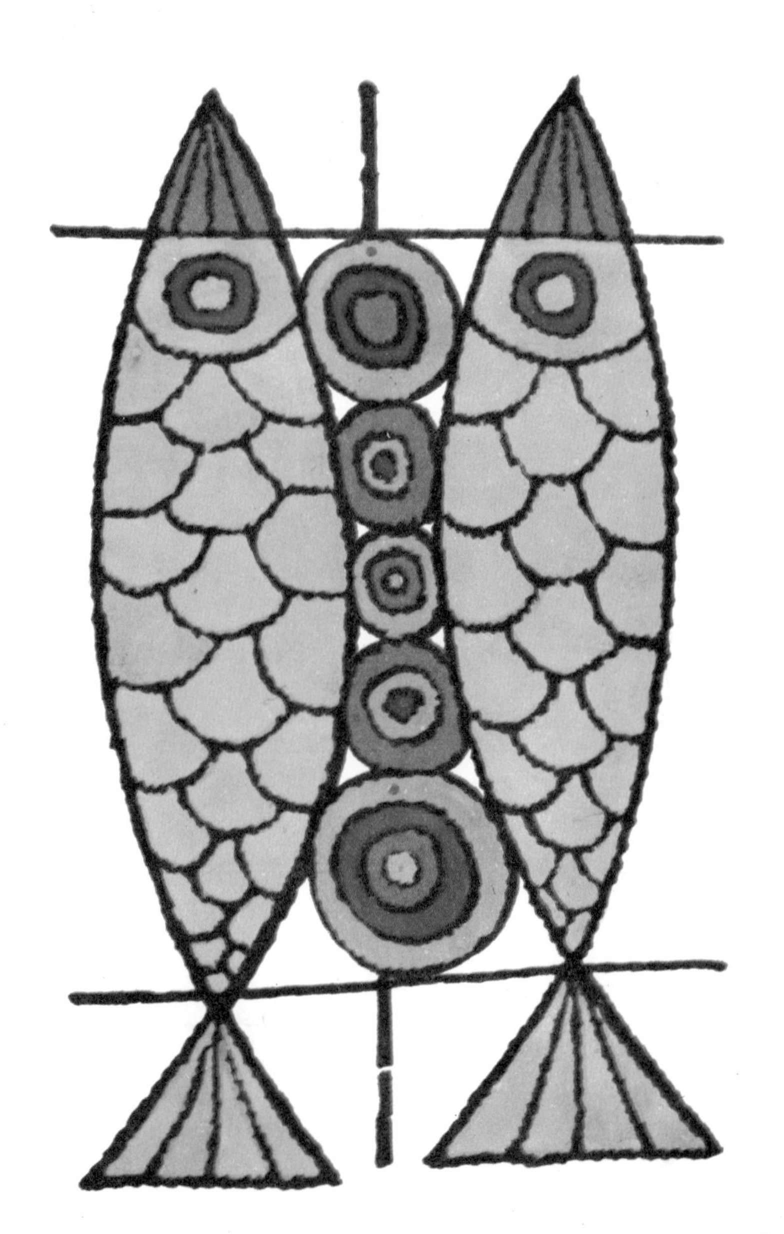

# Flying Lampshade

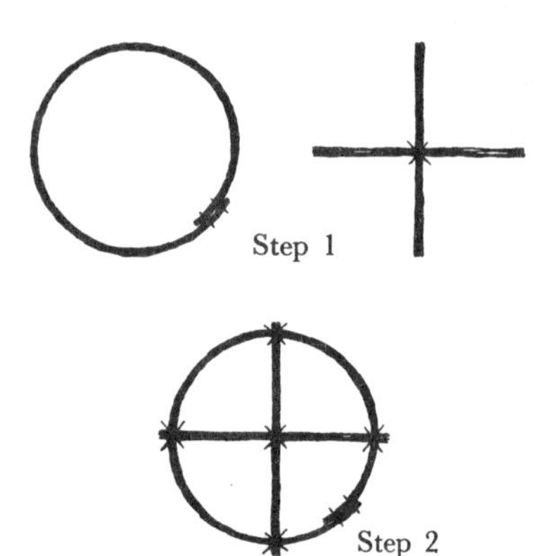


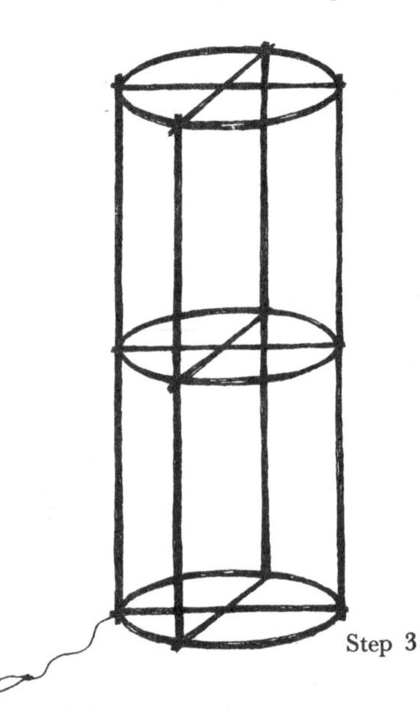


STEP 1: Construct *three* circles from 35″ bamboo strips and *three* crosses from 11″ strips.

STEP 2: Assemble crosses to circles and glue all joints.

STEP 3: Assemble these three components to four 36″ bamboo strips as shown in diagram. Tie the end pieces in first, then center the middle piece in the structure.

STEP 4: Tie a short length of flying line to any one of the end joints and make a loop in the free end (do not make a slip-knot), for later attachment to flying line. Glue all joints.

STEP 5: Cover with rice paper and decorate. Remember that the short string with loop determines the lower end of kite. Do not make decoration upside down!

NOTE: This kite needs no tail, nor does it need a true bridle. The string with loop is merely for convenience. Stability comes from the three-dimensional design.